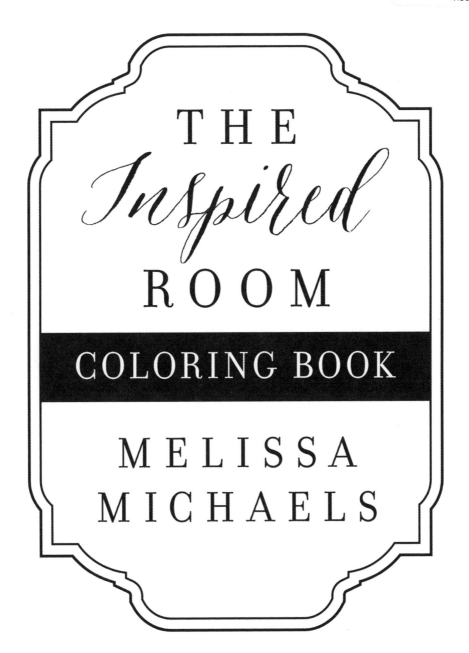

THE *Inspired* ROOM

COLORING BOOK

MELISSA MICHAELS

HARVEST HOUSE PUBLISHERS
EUGENE, OREGON

Scripture quotations are from the Holy Bible, New International Version®, NIV®. Copyright © 1973, 1978, 1984, 2011 by Biblica, Inc.® Used by permission. All rights reserved worldwide.

Cover design and artwork by Nicole Dougherty
Cover image © Galya-art / Shutterstock

Illustrations and lettering by Nicole Dougherty
Home Sweet Home flowers on page 15 © Olga Korneeva / Shutterstock
Floral pattern on page 25 © Maria Galybina / Shutterstock
Tribal pattern on page 75 © Savgraf / Shutterstock

Published in association with the William K. Jensen Literary Agency, 119 Bampton Court, Eugene, Oregon 97404.

The Inspired Room Coloring Book
Copyright © 2016 Melissa Michaels
Published by Harvest House Publishers
Eugene, Oregon 97402
www.harvesthousepublishers.com

ISBN 978-0-7369-6914-7 (pbk.)

Printed in the United States of America

16 17 18 19 20 21 22 23 24 / VP-KC / 10 9 8 7 6 5 4 3

Imagine the Possibilities

These pages provide you with a blank slate—your opportunity to design the home of your dreams. The color palettes you choose and your own unique combinations of textures and patterns can delight your spirit and soothe your active mind. White space and symmetry can bring a sense of order and peace to your inner and outer world, giving your soul room to breathe more deeply. Varying levels of contrast and artful details can further enhance the features you love the most.

Discover what speaks to you through each page and room of the home. As you observe what you find most pleasing to your eye, you will find more clarity in defining and refining your personal style. The pages are perforated and intentionally left blank on the back sides so you can easily tear out your favorites, use the sketches as artwork, or pin them on an inspiration board in your own home.

I hope your time with this book will be a welcome escape from everyday, mundane activities—a way to recharge and rejuvenate your creativity. Dare to try something new. This is a safe place to set aside the rules and stretch the boundaries of the design features you love. Envision cohesive palettes or experiment with the unexpected. It isn't about perfection, but rather delighting in the process.

So find a comfy spot, prepare a relaxing cup of tea, and curl up to begin dreaming of the possibilities. Layer by layer, you'll begin to see a reflection of who you are and what you love!

Share your pages on Instagram with the hashtag #TIRcoloringbook. Follow and tag @theinspiredroom—I'd love to see what you create!

Melissa

Get inspired creating different room layouts!

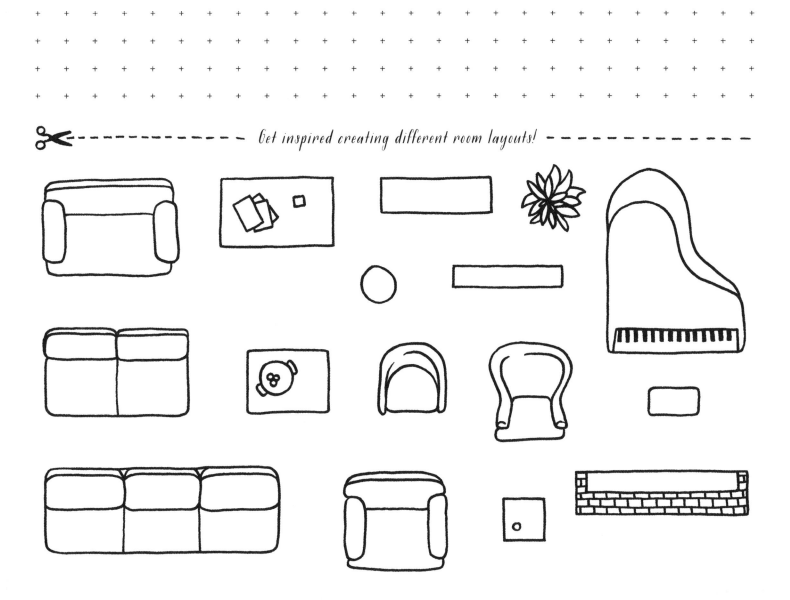

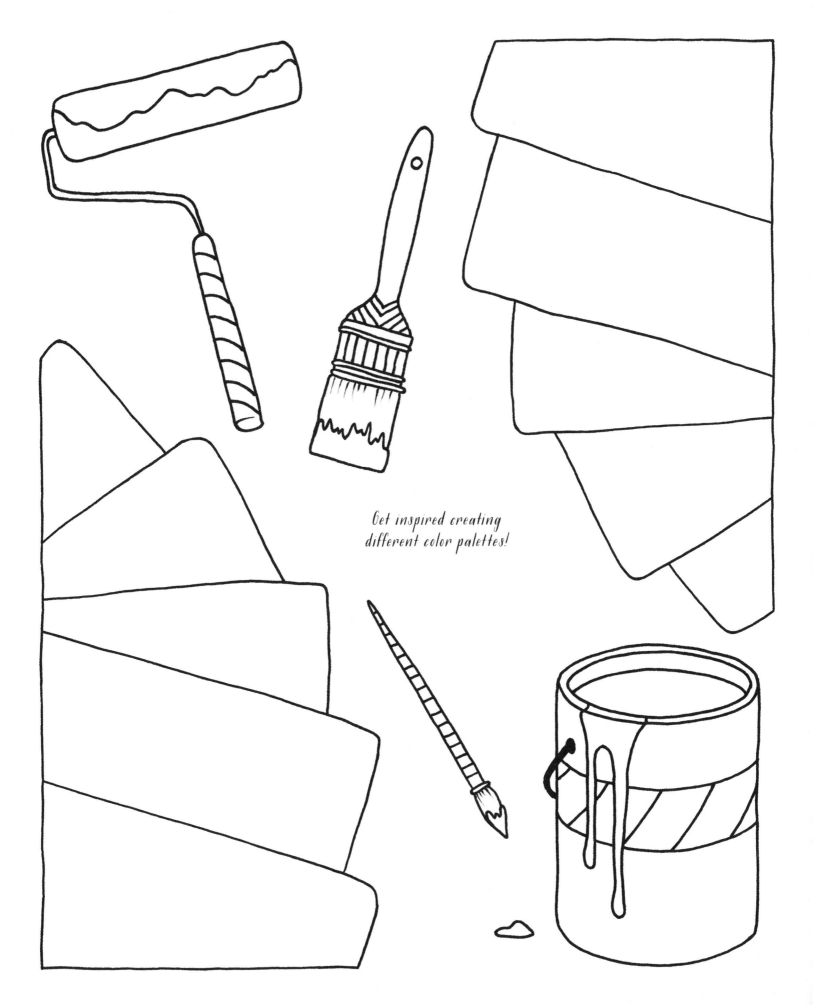

Get inspired creating
different color palettes!

BY
wisdom
A HOUSE IS BUILT,
AND THROUGH
understanding
IT IS ESTABLISHED;
THROUGH
knowledge
ITS ROOMS ARE
FILLED WITH
rare & beautiful
treasures.
PROVERBS 24:3-4

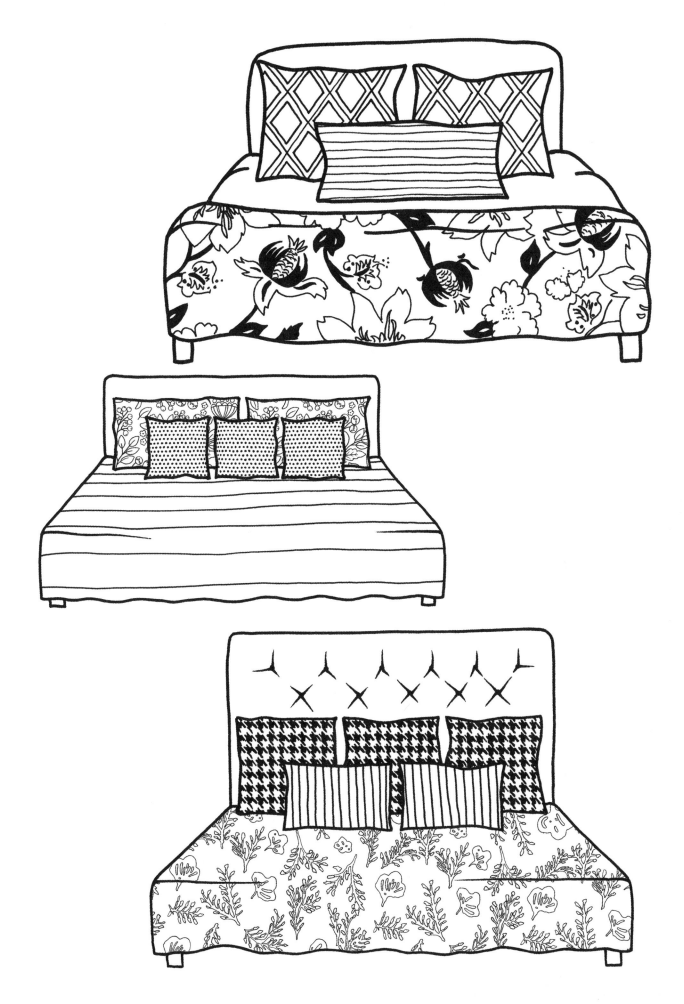

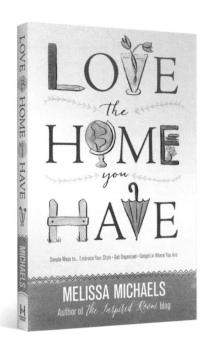
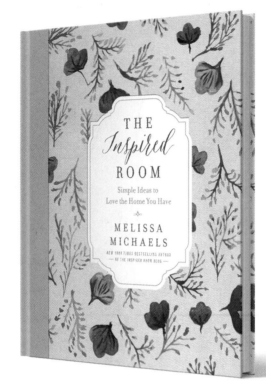

Get Inspiration for Every Room in Your Home

{More helpful resources from Melissa Michaels}

Home decorating is much more than how your furniture is arranged or the pictures you hang on the wall.
It's a reflection of *you*—your style, your family, and the things that matter most in your life.
Let Melissa's books help you create a home that you will love living and entertaining in.

Love the Home You Have,
a *New York Times* Bestseller

- find beauty in the ordinary
- gather inspiration in the 31-day Love Your Home Challenge
- leap from dreamer to doer with confidence

The Inspired Room

- achieve doable improvements for every room
- attain decorating, organizational, and DIY solutions
- learn inspiring ways to think about each room in your home

Make Room for What You Love

- clear out clutter to welcome in what best serves your family
- organize everything from your dishes to your kids with ease
- personalize routines and new habits to simplify your life